THE REAL REASON
FOR CHRISTMAS

Margaret Taliaferro

D0096012

Over the years the celebration of Christmas has grown so commercial that many parents have become alarmed at the lack of spiritual meaning left to the holiday. Here, then, is a reassuring collection of letters designed to be read aloud to a child by his parents or by the child himself, one letter for each of the twelve days of Christmas. Handwritten by the author and illustrated with her line drawings, each selection celebrates the joyful mystery of Christ's birth — THE REAL REASON FOR CHRISTMAS.

Margaret Taliaferro has been teaching children's Bible classes for many years. Each Christmas she has traditionally addressed a letter to her students, presenting the message of the Nativity. This volumn includes twelve of these beloved letters. Although the author is neither a theologian nor a professional artist, she has a rare gift — the ability to instruct and entertain in language that is up to date and warmhearted. (And so simple even an adult can understand!) Whether telling the story of the Magi or discussing the Trinity, the author always brings a light heart and a firm faith to her subject. The result is a charming reaffirmation of the "good news" that is the true meaning of Christmas, and an ideal way for the whole family to rejoice together in this annual message of love.

Margaret Taliaferro is a firm believer in God and God's Word. This book is the result of a growing concern that God's Word often goes unheeded, especially at Christmastime — the holiday when He should be most honored. She is the mother of four children and stepmother of two; her husband is a retired airlines captain.

She is also the author of *Do You Ever Have Questions Like These?* in which she uses the same simple format to explain certain basic Christian tenets to the child.

THE REAL REASON

FOR

CHRISTMAS

FEA Publishing
PO Box 1065
Hobe Sound FL 33475

THE REAL REASON FOR CHRISTMAS

letters to children for the twelve nights of Christmas

by
Margaret Taliaferro

THE REAL REASON FOR CHRISTMAS was originally
published in hardcover by Doubleday &
Company, Inc. in 1977.
Paperback, Doubleday-Galilee original 1982

ISBN: 0-9618730-0-0
Library of Congress Catalog Card Number 87-090171

Library of Congress Cataloging in Publication Data

Taliaferro, Margaret.
  The Real Reason For Christmas

To
my young friends in
the Long Island class
for whom these letters
were   first   written.

Margaret Taliaferro

THE REAL REASON

FOR

CHRISTMAS

from Mrs.T. ___

To You

1ˢᵗ letter

Dear

I wonder if you are busy
Christmas shopping now – going

up   and   down

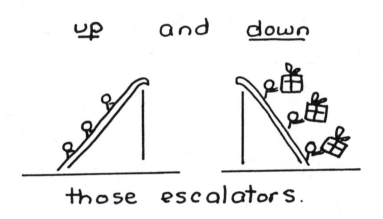

those escalators.

If you are, I hope that
you will remember at the
same time that Jesus Christ
is the _real_ reason for
Christmas.

And there is a great deal to think about concerning Jesus Christ. Do you know, for example, that He didn't actually start to be Jesus on that first Christmas Day?

No, He always was. It was just that at a certain point in time God chose to break through history and to send His only Son down from heaven to earth.

Now, perhaps you've sometimes wondered about heaven_

What is it like?

Who is there?

Well, here are some of the facts that the Bible tells us about heaven —

No
tears in
heaven

No
time in
heaven

No
sickness in
heaven

No darkness  in heaven

And the Bible says that heaven is better than anything we've ever—

<u>seen</u> on earth—

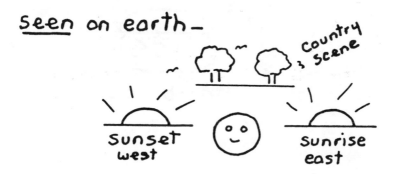

<u>heard</u> on earth—

<u>done</u> on earth—

ball game   tennis

ski   skate   swim

hamburger

<u>thought</u> <u>of</u> or <u>dreamed</u> <u>of</u> on earth—

happy times   games   fun times

God and Jesus Christ and God's Holy Spirit are there and there is love forever in heaven.

Well, then, since heaven is so wonderful, why do you suppose that Jesus Christ left there to come to earth?

The answer to that is:

God so loves the world (and that includes you and me today) that He wants us all to be with Him forever. But in order for us to be with God we have

to be as perfect as He is. And
no matter how hard we try,
we just can't make ourselves
perfect. It's like this —

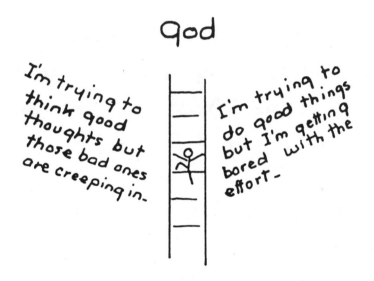

God

I'm trying to think good thoughts but those bad ones are creeping in.

I'm trying to do good things but I'm getting bored with the effort —

We just can't get all the way
up that ladder on our own.
And that is why God sent His
only Son, Jesus Christ, from

heaven to earth. Then Jesus, when He was a man on earth, took all of our bad thoughts and deeds to the cross _for us_. So now, those of us who believe in Him need _never_ _ever_ be separated from God.

So, you see, Jesus left heaven to _save_ _us_. And we should always remember this and thank Him - especially at Christmas time. Will you?

Lots of love,

Mrs. T.

from Mrs.T. ≡ 🙂

To You

2nd letter

Dear

Have you ever stopped to think that no one can be <u>very</u> <u>very</u> sure of what's going to happen next? Even the <u>next</u> <u>day</u>? Even the <u>next</u> <u>minute</u>?

will I win the prize?

will I have fun at the party?

will there be ice cream for supper?

will my friend telephone me today?

?

Yes, we have lots of everyday

questions like:

who _____?
what_____?
why _____?
how _____?
where _____?

But do you know that there were no questions like these in the life of Jesus? God told the people _way_ _ahead_ of time about Jesus. He answered those questions in this way:

who?
Jesus Christ, the

Son of god.

What?
He would come to
earth. And He would
make -
   the poor people happy,
      😊

   the sad people glad,
      😊

   the blind people see,
      😳

   and the sick people well.

Why?
He would come to

save the people ✝

How?

He would come by
way of a miracle
birth to a girl who
wasn't yet married.

Where?

He would be born in the
town of Bethlehem.

You can find all these
promises in the part of the
Bible called the Old Testament,
and they were written by
certain of God's chosen

people _hundreds_ (and sometimes _thousands_) of years
before the birth of Jesus Christ.

Now, wouldn't you think that
when Jesus was born, everyone would have said,"Oh yes,
this _is_ the Son of God, we
know that, because we
already know the answers
to _who_ and _what_ and _why_
and _how_ and _where_"?

But they _didn't_ say that.
They didn't believe at all.

_It_ was sort of like a

picture puzzle.

And it wasn't until after Jesus had died and had come back to life that certain people said, "Oh yes, of course, now we see that He truly _was_ the Son of God."

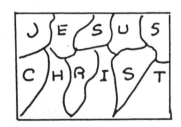

But now, you and I can look way back and way ahead in the Bible, and we can read about the coming of Jesus Christ throughout it all. So we have

NO EXCUSE

We should believe, with no doubts at all, that He truly _was_ the Son of God.

I do—

Do _you_?

I hope very much that you <u>do</u>.

Lots of love,

Mrs. T.

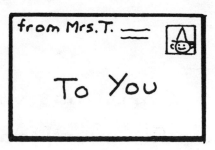

from Mrs. T. ≈

TO YOU

3<u>rd</u> letter

Dear

    Isn't Christmas vacation fun, when every day seems like Saturday — you can sleep late in the morning, and you don't have to worry about the homework that you have to do each night?

    And isn't it fun, too, to plan for Christmas — the presents, the good times, the parties? And yet, in the midst of it all, I hope that you'll sometimes stop to think of this:

How strange it is that
  the shops are so crowded—
  the windows are so decor-
  ated—
  the streets are so lit up—
  the people are so busy—

all   because   of one little
baby   born   almost 2000
years   ago—

  who lived in a very small
  country—
  who   had no money of

His own —
who never went to college —
who never led an army —
who never ran for public
office —
who never fired a gun —

And did you know too that
He had to —

borrow a boat when He went
out on the lake —
and borrow a donkey when
He had to ride —
and His mother borrowed a
manger for Him when He was born —
and His friends borrowed a

tomb for Him when He died—

BUT—

<u>No</u> <u>one</u> has ever changed history as <u>He</u> did — and we date our calendar from His short life.

B.C. — A.D.

Now, when —in a few short weeks— you start writing the new year on your school papers, it won't be because a lot of smart people got together and said:

No, it will be because it's
that number of years since

the birth of Jesus Christ.

How come?

Well, you see, that borrowed tomb needed only to be borrowed because He was in it for such a short time. On Easter morning it was empty again, and during the next few weeks Jesus was seen alive by over 500 people at one time (once He even built a fire for a beach picnic with His friends).

So, if there hadn't been an

Easter, there wouldn't be a Christmas. And what would the world be like without Christmas?

NO FUN

So, on Christmas Day, remember to thank God for sending His Son, Jesus Christ, to earth — especially for you. He died for all the naughty things you and I —

did —
do —
will do —

and if we say we're sorry to

God, and if we believe that Jesus Christ is our savior, then we live on ⎯⎯⟶ and

on ⎯⎯⟶ and on ⎯⎯⟶ and on

forever with God.

And when we're with God, every day is Christmas Day.

Lots of love,

Mrs. T.

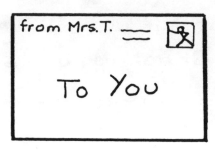

from Mrs. T. ═

To You

4<u>th</u> letter

Dear

These days and weeks
before Christmas are fun,
aren't they? They're a time
when we hide presents
in the backs of closets
where no one is allowed
to peek.

Yes, it's a time to keep

secrets. Yet do you know that the very _first_ Christmas secret _ and the greatest one in all the world _ was kept by Mary, the mother of Jesus?

An angel told her the secret. It was that she would give birth to the baby Jesus by the Holy Spirit of God. Now Mary was going to marry Joseph, a carpenter from the town of Nazareth but, as they were not yet married, Mary wondered _

How could this be?

How could she have a baby?

The angel explained that it wouldn't be a usual sort of birth. This would be a super-natural(a more than natural)event. What a shock for Mary, who was probably no more than a teen-ager at the time. Here she was — not only talking to an angel (a fact that was just as out of the ordinary then as it would be today) but this angel was giving her the most startling news.

And then, I wonder, <u>where</u>
was Mary when the angel
appeared? What was she
doing?

cooking?
washing dishes?
sweeping?
sewing?
out in the garden
        weeding?
or was it bedtime
and she hadn't quite
        gone to sleep?

I wonder— don't you?

Now for us, looking back, Mary is honored, and we think of her as being very blessed. But during those months before the birth of Jesus, she wasn't honored at all. There must have been a great deal of gossip, and surely people embarrassed her many times. Yet, in spite of all this, Mary didn't go around trying to explain everything — instead, the Bible says, she just "thought about all these things in her heart."

Can <u>you</u> keep a secret? Or do you go around saying everything to everyone?

Sometimes God asks us to be very quiet and just to think about things in our hearts.

But, now, what if Mary had said "No" to that angel? She could have said, "I don't want to be the mother of God's Son. It's too scarey, too different. I want to be like everyone else." If she *had* said that, would Jesus have come into the world?

Yes, He would have because it was in the plan of God to send His Son into the world to save the people (including you and me) from their sins. But then *some* *other* girl, rather than Mary, would have received the blessing.

Of course we know that Mary didn't say "No."

She said, "I am God's servant. I will do anything that He wishes."

Mary wasn't a rich girl nor was she an important girl according to the world's standards. She wasn't a princess, or the daughter of the mayor of Nazareth. But

she was a girl who was
willing and ready to
say "Yes" to God, what-
ever the cost.

Are _you_ ready to say
"Yes" if you're called by
God to be different? Or are
you more apt to say, "No,
I'd rather be like every-
one else"?

They're having
more fun over
there. I'd rather
say "No" to God
and join them.

I do hope that you'll never be like that. I hope that you'll always be ready with a "Yes" for God.

Lots of love,

Mrs. T.

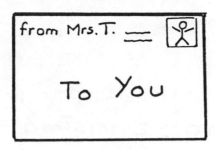

from Mrs.T. ══ 🧍

To You

5th letter

Dear

Are you busy just now putting Christmas decorations all around your house? Your room?

Well, if you are, I hope that you will sometimes take time

out to read the Christ-
mas story.

And when you come
to the part about the
birth of Jesus, be sure
to notice how very dif-
ferent <u>His</u> birth was
from yours.

You were born in a

hospital where it's_

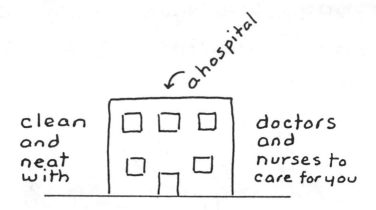

↙ a hospital

clean
and
neat
with

doctors
and
nurses to
care for you

Jesus was born in a
stable where it was _

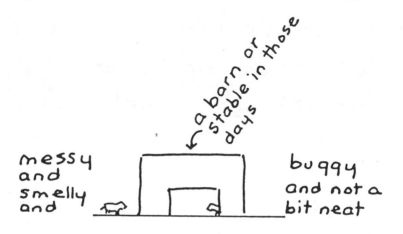

↙ a barn or
stable in those
days

messy
and
smelly
and

buggy
and not a
bit neat

God <u>chose</u> the stable. He could have chosen a palace with a queen as mother of the baby.

Now, why do you think that Jesus' birthplace was a dirty barn, and His mother just an ordinary girl? I think God arranged it that way to show us that He looks at the world far differently than we do. Kings and queens in palaces are, to Him, just the same as you and I. And Mary, a very ordinary girl, was chosen by Him because her heart belonged to Him.

And then too, as you read the story, maybe you'll notice someone who seems to be not-so-important, and yet, who is really <u>very</u> special and <u>very</u> important.

It is Joseph—

You see, just as Mary was chosen to be the

mother of God's Son, so too was Joseph chosen for a part. God wanted him to be the step-father (God was the heavenly father but Joseph was to be Jesus' father on earth). God's plan was:

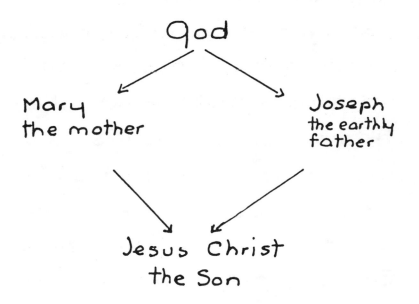

God

Mary
the mother

Joseph
the earthly
father

Jesus Christ
the Son

Then notice, too, in the Christmas story that there was no room in the town for Mary to have the baby.

It was Joseph on that long ago night in Bethlehem who knocked on all the doors of the houses saying something like this: "My wife is having a baby and she's very tired. We've traveled a long distance. Do you have a room for us?"

And in each case the answer was:

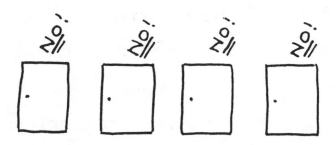

Finally, Joseph found an inn (an inn is like a motel) with a stable be-hind it where there <u>was</u> room. And, as you know, that stable is where the baby Jesus was born.

Now, I wonder what

the people at the inn were doing that night—

Eating?
Drinking?
Having a party?

They didn't know that out in the dark, un-comfortable barn a baby was coming into the world and that the world, through Him, would be completely changed.

No one knew—
No one cared—

But I hope that, if you had been at the inn that night, you would have somehow known the difference. Maybe then you would have gone out to the barn and invited them to come into your room at the inn.

Do you think that you would have?

Perhaps, at this point, you might say, "Well, Joseph has done a very good job and that's about it, as far as he's con-cerned."

But not at all —

Because shortly after the birth of Jesus, a very big problem suddenly appeared.

Here is what happened. There was this very angry king who first heard about Jesus from three wise men. He was so cross — that king—

and so scared that the baby might some day be king in his place, that he decided to do something about it.

"I'll just order all the babies in Bethlehem killed— that'll do it," he said, and he gave the order to his soldiers.

But —

That wasn't at all in the plan of God.

"<u>My</u> thoughts are higher than <u>your</u> thoughts," says God in the Bible, and that goes for kings' thoughts as well as for your and my thoughts.

here are god's thoughts → God

and here are people's thoughts ↳

click   click   click   click

So, you see, that bad king didn't have his way. God spoke to Joseph in a dream and told him to take Mary and the baby Jesus to another country. They were to stay there until the death of that very annoying king.

Now, when Joseph woke from that dream, he could have said, "What a silly old dream that was. And, anyway, I like it here— I don't want to move." But he didn't. He obeyed god and the life of the baby Jesus was saved.

So now, as Christmas draws near, let's think about all this—

of Mary, who was willing to serve the Lord—

of Joseph, who was willing to obey the Lord—

and of the birth of the

baby in a stable be-
cause there was no
room at the inn.

Lots of love,

Mrs. T.

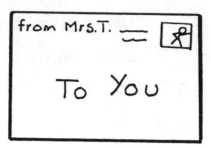

from Mrs. T. ⸺

To You

6th letter

Dear

It's getting very close to Christmas, and I wonder now if you're taking time from all your busy-ness to think about the reason <u>behind</u>—

the presents

the tree

the parties

the food

Because the reason behind it all is that it's Jesus' birthday.

I hope that you're reading about it in your Bible. And when you do, be sure to notice everything very carefully. Don't just whip through and say, "There—now I know all about that," because actually there's a great deal to think about.

Take, for instance, those shepherds. If _you_ had been there that night, imagine your surprise to see the sky suddenly lit up — and to hear beautiful beings from another world all singing in harmony about "peace on earth." Yes, those shepherds — and the sheep too — must have been completely shocked and amazed at the sight. Then, too, did they wonder (as maybe you are now) why the angels sang of "peace on earth"?

Is there peace on earth?

Has there ever been peace

on earth? What does that mean?

There has been so much fighting, and there have been so many wars. And then, we must admit that sometimes we fight among ourselves, don't we? How about you — with your brothers and sisters, and with some of your friends?

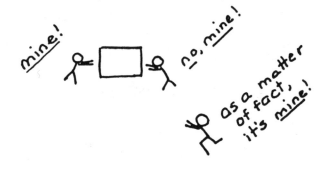

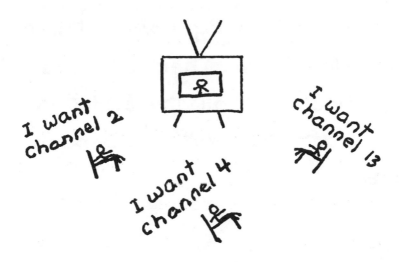

But then it all appears
clear to us when we
realize that this peace
has to come first to
the heart of each person.
Jesus Christ came to earth
in order that He might take
away all those bad things

if we are truly sorry that we did them. Then all that fighting and all the bad things are forgiven and are gone forever.

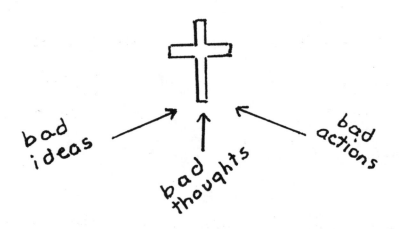

bad ideas

bad thoughts

bad actions

Then the peace that the angels sang about would mean that there's no longer that tug-of-war going on inside.

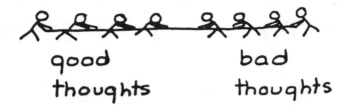

good thoughts   bad thoughts

Peace, through Christ, with no more tugging and pulling. Think of that when you read the Bible story.

And if you _had_ been in the fields with the shepherds that night, let's hope that you'd have gone with them to Bethlehem. Then

you would have been one
of the first people on
earth _actually_ _to_ _see_
the Son of God, the baby
Jesus.

Lots of love,

Mrs.T.

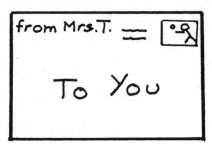

7th letter

Dear

Very soon now it will be Christmas Day, and there will be lots of presents to give and to get. But I wonder if you know that at the first Christmas, the baby Jesus received presents too. They didn't exactly arrive on time but, then, don't you some- times receive a present <u>after</u> Christmas because it came from so far away and because the mail is so slow?

Of course, Jesus' presents weren't the same sort as yours. I'm quite sure, for example, that you haven't put gold and frankincense and myrrh on the top of your Christmas list.

gold
frankincense
myrrh
bicycle
toys
watch
games

But actually, for the birth

of the Son of God, these
three presents had deep
meanings:

gold—
   for Christ the King of
   the world.
frankincense—
   for Christ the Son of God.
myrrh—
   for Christ who came to
   die for us.

Now, who were the people
who brought these presents?

They were wise men, early

scientists, who studied the stars and the planets _ and they came from a country far to the east of Israel.

One night while searching the stars they discovered a new and brilliant star, like a comet or meteor. When they saw this they knew it was super-natural (more than natural) and that it surely meant the birth of a most unusual person.

Immediately those very wise men prepared their

presents and set off to find out more about this important event. Now, what would <u>you</u> do if you were following a star_ low and bright in the sky?

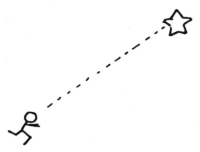

Once you'd arrived in the land over which it hung, you'd go to see the king of that land, wouldn't you? After all, you'd reason, this baby is of such importance that he must surely be in the palace.

Well, that's just what the wise men did. But once there, they found nothing but a furious and angry king. You see, when this king heard about another and far more important king, he went into a panic. If the skies changed at the birth of this baby, here was no ordinary person, decided this king.

And, as a matter of fact, he was very right, wasn't he? Because stars don't appear and disappear according to the reigns of kings — nor, for example, do they announce elections here in the United States.

Our newspapers don't look like this on Election Day —

A star such as that one has never appeared since the birth of Christ. And the evil king on that long ago day, recognizing the threat of it, declared that he would kill the baby.

Yes, but _you_ _can't_ _fight_ _against_ _the_ _sure_ _and_ _certain_ _plan_ _of_ _god._ And His plan was that Christ might come to earth to save all those who would believe in Him.

Now, the star led the wise men to the town of Bethlehem, where they found the baby.

They gave their presents, and then the Bible tells us that they worshipped Him. They were very wise, those men, because they hadn't worshipped the _palace_ king. You see, they knew the difference. True royalty was there in a manger in Bethlehem_ not on a throne in

Jerusalem.

not on a throne

but in a manger

And then they went home. They took a different route to confuse that scheming king. It was all explained to them by God through.

a dream—and so it was in this way that the life of the baby Jesus was spared—

God protects His own.

In the Bible you can read all about those early scientists and of their presents to Jesus. And as you do, you might at the same time think of His present to us. It's so big — that present— that the whole world is changed because of it.

It's <u>His</u> <u>life</u> and it's such a wonderful present that even the stars moved their positions in the sky when He came to earth to give it.

Think of <u>that</u> wonderful miracle of the skies when next you're out on a star-lit night.

Lots of love,

Mrs. T.

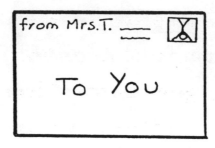

from Mrs.T. ___ 🗙

To You

8ᵗʰ letter

Dear

Are you busy Christmas shopping? And have you made a list to help you fit the presents to the people? If you have, maybe your people-list looks something like this.

Mom
Dad
sister
brother
best friend
2nd best friend
3rd best friend (if he gives me one)

But now, there's someone who is <u>not</u> on that list yet wants a very special present from you.

<u>Who</u> is it?
It's Jesus —
And <u>what</u> does He want?
He wants your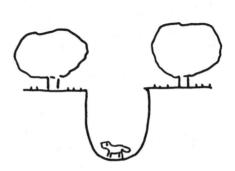

When Jesus was a man on earth He said:

"the foxes
have holes

the birds
have nests

but the Son of God has
nowhere to lay his head."

Think of that ⸺

no <u>room</u> as you have ⸺
no <u>house</u> as you have ⸺
no <u>things</u> as you have ⸺

Yet <u>without</u> all of that,
He was still the richest

man on earth _ because
He had so much love.

And then He has a pres-
ent for you each Christmas.

Do you know what it is?
His <u>love</u> and His <u>life</u> for you.

He gave you this pres-
ent long ago on that first
Christmas night. There were
very few that night who
knew the truth about it
all _ only His mother Mary,
and Joseph her husband,
and some shepherds who

had come in from the fields. The other people had all crowded into Bethlehem to be registered (or counted) and to pay taxes to the government.

It was a noisy time in Bethlehem just then, even as Christmas is a noisy time in New York City or Atlanta or Denver — or any other city.

Bethlehem was very crowded and the people were busy and tired, and no one could be bothered to go out to peek through the door of a certain stable. Who cared? The important thing was to get the money paid and to stick with the crowd.

crowds and money

Yes, it was noisy in the streets and in the houses, but it was very quiet in the stable. No busy-ness there, no collecting of money. Just a baby being born. But from that day on, the world has never been the same.

And if they'd had newspapers then, what do you think the next day's news would have been—

front page like this—

or,

front page like this—

Those people didn't know the truth, or care about it, but _you_ know and I'm sure that you care. So remember this important present on Christmas Day.

You won't see it under your
tree
or in your stocking,
but you'll find it in your
heart
if you ask the Lord Jesus in.

Lots of love,

Mrs. T.

from Mrs. T. ═

To You

9th letter

Dear

Did you ever stop to think how strange it is that God— the maker of the earth, the sky, the universe, and us— should have sent His only Son <u>into</u> <u>the</u> <u>world</u>? And, because it's such a strange and amazing event, wouldn't you think that the whole world would have welcomed Him? After all, His coming was spoken of many times in the Bible (as a matter of fact, it even says there that He'd

be born in the town of
Bethlehem).

Yes, once in all of history,
God's Son came to earth as
a man, yet no one was
there to greet Him. In fact,
there was no room for
Him at the inn in Bethlehem,
when Joseph was looking
for a place to spend the
night.

And, thinking of this
no-welcome scene, wouldn't
you expect then that God
would have said, "Forget

it," and would have removed the baby Jesus from that stable in Bethlehem?

At any time during the birth and the life and the death of Jesus, God could have said, "No – stop – I do not want my Son to go through this – the people are not worth it."

We know from the Bible that Jesus at the cross could have called on ten thousand angels. And of course, if He could have done that at the cross, He could have done it at any other time during His life as well.

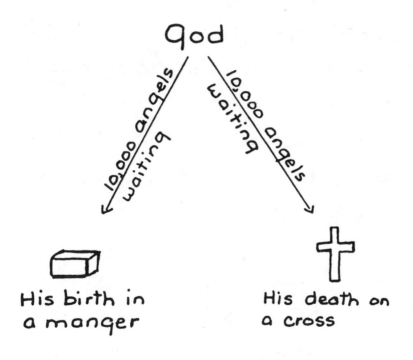

god

10,000 angels waiting

10,000 angels waiting

His birth in a manger

His death on a cross

Now, if God had sent those angels into action,

Jesus would have been spared the cross.

BUT_ if <u>that</u> had happened the world would have been lost, and you and I would be very <u>un</u>safe right now.

Maybe we can think of it by using a scale. In other words, it was either this_

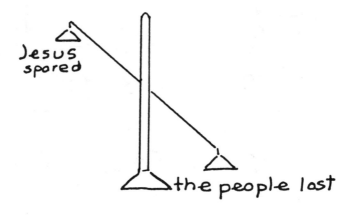

Jesus spared

the people lost

or this—

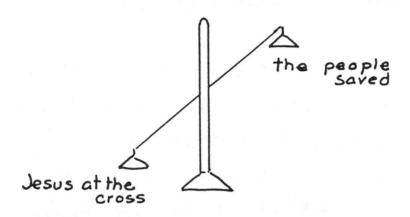

the people saved

Jesus at the cross

But what exactly can we be saved _from_ ?

The Bible says that Jesus came "to save His people from their sins." Well, to that we might say, "It's O.K. for all those sinning people way back then _but who needs it now?"

And to answer that we have to think about sin and what it is.

First of all, it's all those bad things like killing and stealing. Yes, we know all that. But then, it's all those little, sneaky things like_

hatred_

    😕 <u>I don't</u> , 🧍
        like him

jealousy—
envy—

☹ ——I wish I——→ 🧍
were more like him

anger—

☹ ——grrrr——→ 🧍
he burns me up

Sin also means the act
of not thinking about God—
paying no attention to God—
the sin of saying, "I'm
doing all right— who needs
God?"

Have you ever noticed

that the middle letter of
the   word "SIN" is I ?
And so, if I put myself
in the middle or center
of my life, it's a <u>sin</u>.

me
S ⚲ N
myself
I

Looking at it that way,
we're all on that scale
together, aren't we? And
we all need to be saved.

So this Christmas, let's

especially thank Jesus for coming into the world and for <u>not</u> calling those ten thousand angels. Let's thank Him for saving us and let's welcome Him into our hearts.

Lots of love,

Mrs.T.

from Mrs.T. 〜〜 🙂

To You

10th letter

Dear

    I wonder what you're doing and especially what you're thinking about. Right now I know that Christmas is an important part of your thoughts and that you're very busy planning the presents you're going to give and thinking about the ones you're going to get.

    Well, I'm doing the

same thing here.

But, while we're going through this busy time, let's try to think most of all of that first Christmas and about the birth of Jesus Christ.

And when you read about it in the Bible, notice especially what the angel said to the shepherds out in the fields on that very important night. First, he told them that they mustn't be afraid.

Now, why should grown men __be__ afraid?

Because, without god, __any__ thing different __can__ be scarey. Yet __with__ god, there's nothing to fear— that's why the angel said, "Don't be afraid."

And god says the same thing today.

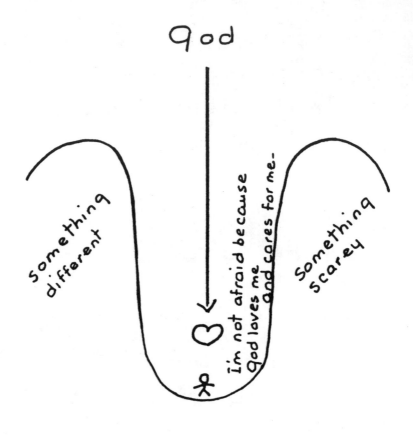

Next, the angel said that he had the most wonderful news for them — the very best —

"A savior has been born for you tonight in Bethlehem."

A <u>savior</u> — what's a savior?

It must mean some-one who <u>saves</u>, don't you think?

The baby Jesus, born to save.

But from <u>what</u>?

And <u>how</u>?

Well, if someone is in the deep water and can't swim, he needs to be saved, doesn't he?

HELP!

Someone saves him

Now, this is how Jesus saves people:

HELP! I'm sorry for all the bad things I've done, Lord Jesus, please save me.

Jesus

Jesus saves him by tak-
ing all those bad things
on to Himself on the cross.

And He came "for you"
the angel told the
shepherds, and that
means for <u>you</u> too today and <u>every</u> day
forever. Jesus is God's
Christmas present to you.

Now, as for those
presents that you <u>can</u>
see, you don't leave
them all wrapped up
under the tree, do you?

No, you—

accept them and open them.
Why don't you accept
god's present to you?
Here's the result if you
do:

Lots of love,
    Mrs. T.

from Mrs.T. ══ 🖼️

To You

11th letter

Dear

Christmas time is great fun, isn't it? Parties, and presents, and school vacations, and holly wreaths, and Christmas trees all make it very exciting.

And yet, we should never forget that Christmas is really Christ's birthday. It's a time to look back through our reading of the Bible to that first Christmas. And as we do, we find that then there were no —

parties to give—

presents to buy —
wreaths to hang —
trees to trim —
vacations to take from
school —

   just a very quiet, very
un-noticed birth of a baby
in a stable.

   But, down through the ages,
this particular birth has proven
to be the most important e-
vent that the world has ever
known. So, you see, we can
look back on all this in wonder.

But now, here's something else to think about: do you know that we can look ahead in wonder too?

And do you know _why_?

Because Jesus Christ is coming back to the earth again. Yes, He is coming again — this time to make a new earth. Won't that be wonderful? It will be a beautiful new earth where, the Bible tells us, the big animals will no longer eat the little animals be- cause they will all be the best of friends.

lamb   lion

And do you wonder now
<u>when</u> this will happen?

Tomorrow at lunch time?
A week from next Monday?
The first sunny day in June?
10, or 100, or 100,000 years from
now?

No one knows. God will choose

the time. Actually, it's like
this :

Jesus   Christ

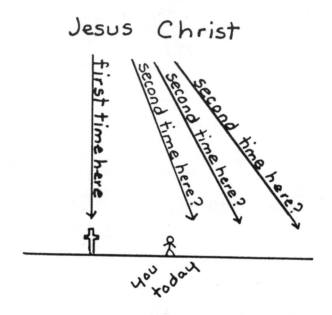

So now, in case this happens
soon, how can we get ready-

buy a new dress?

buy a new suit?

buy a new pair of
sneakers in order to
run around that new
earth ?

take a bath daily
in order to be very
clean ?

get higher marks in school?

No, there's only one way to be ready for Jesus Christ's next appearance — and that is to open your heart to Him. You have to get out of the center of your life and invite Jesus to come into the center.

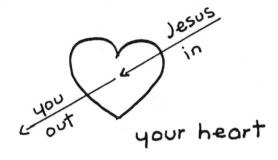

In that way, you'll <u>always</u> be ready.

And so, <u>this</u> Christmas let's thank God for sending His Son, Jesus, on that first Christmas Day, and let's be ready for the wonder-ful Second Coming of Jesus, whenever that might be—

Lots of love,

Mrs. T.

from Mrs. T. == ☺

To You

12th letter

Dear

  If you wake up on Christmas morning feeling like this:

whee - I especially love the world today

I hope you'll remember that.

God is love
and
God loves you.

Merry Christmas and lots
of love,
                    Mrs. T.